AFFAIR WITH THE WORDS

WORDS ARE THE ECSTATIC LOVE OF A POET.

SANA PAUL

Copyright © Sana Paul
All Rights Reserved.

This book has been published with all efforts taken to make the material error-free after the consent of the author. However, the author and the publisher do not assume and hereby disclaim any liability to any party for any loss, damage, or disruption caused by errors or omissions, whether such errors or omissions result from negligence, accident, or any other cause.

While every effort has been made to avoid any mistake or omission, this publication is being sold on the condition and understanding that neither the author nor the publishers or printers would be liable in any manner to any person by reason of any mistake or omission in this publication or for any action taken or omitted to be taken or advice rendered or accepted on the basis of this work. For any defect in printing or binding the publishers will be liable only to replace the defective copy by another copy of this work then available.

THE STRENGTH ALL OF US HOLD AND THE COURAGE
MAKES US BOLD,

TO FACE THE CHALLENGES, AND LOVE OURSELVES
WITHOUT CONDITIONS

EMERGES THE THOUGHT FROM THE TREE OF LIFE.

To all my readers and especially to Satyam

Contents

Contents

Contents

Foreword

life needs stories and few cosmic theories to become the universal.

Preface

IT'S BEEN A LONG TIME SINCE I WAS THINKING TO COMPILE ALL OF MY POEMS .THIS BOOK COMPRISES OF MOST OF THE POEMS I HAVE WRITTEN SO FAR. I WROTE THESE POEMS AT DIFFRENT PHASES OF MY LIFE WITH DIFFRENT SET OF EMOTIONS. I DEEPLY BELEIVE IN THE ESTACTIC NATURE OF THE WORDS THE CONNECTION, THEY CREATE BETWEEEN HUMANS AND THE IMPACT THEY HAVE ON THE MINDSET OF PEOPLE.THE PURE AND HONEST WORDS GIVE BIRTH TO SUBTLE AND TRUE EMOTIONS. BEAUTIFUL WORDS HAVE THE CAPABILITY TO MAP A STRONG MIND. I HOPE READERS ARE ABLE TO RELATE TO MY POEMS AND RECONNECT TO MY WORK.

Acknowledgements

I WOULD LIKE TO THANK MY FRIENDS AND FAMILY FOR THE SUPPORT AND ADMIRATION. MY TEACHERS HAVE A GREAT ROLE IN BUILDING THE CREATIVE SPHERE OF MY MIND, EVERTHING WAS POSSIBLE BECAUSE OF THE STRENGTH AND COURAGE THEY IMBIBED ME WITH.

THANKS TO MY MOTHER RAFIA GANI AND DR SUSHIL RAZDAN FOR IMMENSE ENCOURAGMENT.

I WOULD LIKE TO OFFER MY SPECIAL THANKS TO MY GRANDPARENTS AND MY PARENTS , Mr. FEROZE ANHEMD PAUL AND Mrs. AFROZA FOR THEIR LOVE AND CARE.

IT WILL BE WHOLLY INCOMPLETE WITHOUT INVOLVING MY BEST FRIENDS FAIZA MALIK, MADIHA, SAUSON, ANDLEEB

FOREMOST I WOULD LIKE TO THANK Mr. SHIBA GHOSH SIR FOR ENCOURAGING ME TO PUBLISH MY WORK.

AND ALL THANKS TO MY LITTLE LOVED ONES LILY, AISHE AND AL-SUDAIS.

OFFERING MY GRATITUDE TO THE EFFORTS OF Mr. SATYAM SHARMA FOR MAKING ME REALIZE MY POTENTIAL.

THANK YOU EVERYONE.

Prologue

THESE POEMS HAVE BEEN COMPILED TO GIVE WORDS TO THE EMOTIONS OF PEOPLE WHO ARE NOT ABLE TO EXPRESS THEMSELVES. AND ARE NOT ABLE TO CONNECT TO THEIR TRUE FEELINGS. "THE TREE OF LIFE WITH THE BLOSSOM FROM HEAVENS ENCAPTURES THE WORDS FROM A PAINFUL HEART". THESE POEMS ARE INSPIRATION BASED AND WORK OF FICTION IS ALSO INVOLVED.

1. THE LITTLE RAINDROPS

When the rain felt from the sky and gave some drops to ocean.

It touched the heart of blossoms,

It played the tune of flutes.

When the raindrops merged with ocean water.

It giggled full of smile.

It played with flower petals and tried to sway into bays.

But never knew those little drops they are in a huge ocean.

As falling from sky might have been a joy...

But now they felt fearfull and missed that sky,

But the huge ocean never let them stay at a place.

It swayed them up and down, put them above and over...

Miserable raindrops always felt scared.

They sighed full of pain...

And one day, Ocean was full of rage.

It stormed...and raindrops were put in a cage.

Then came the sun, and it sucked their soul,

And took there bodies along...

AH! it was full of pain.

In their eyes SUN found their longing for moon.

And their desperate desire for sky...

So Sun took their souls high and merged their bodies.
Now for once again a cloud was made with same raindrops....
They watched the ocean and thanked the sky for the beloved
MOON,
They danced in sky and singed together every noon.

2. THE TOXIC CROWD -THE THINGS THEY WILL KEEP TELLING TO YOU

THEY WILL TELL YOU, YOUR FACE IS SO UGLY.
THEY WILL ALWAYS BE AND EVERYWHERE,
THERE FOR YOU TO BULLY.
THEY WILL TELL YOU, YOUR BODY IS SO FAT.
THEY MIGHT EVEN SAY YOU LOOK THIN AS A RAT.
THEY MIGHT SAY YOU ARE FAIR JUST LIKE THAT
WHITE CAT.
THEY MAY EVEN SAY YOU LOOK AS BLACK AS A BAT.
BUT YOU DON'T NEED TO BELEIVE THEM.
THEY WILL COME TO SAY YOU...HII!
BUT SET YOURSELF FREE AND TELL THEM..BYE!
BECAUSE...THEY WANT TO PUT SHACKLES IN YOUR
ARMS.
THEY WANT TO GIVE YOUR SOUL TO STORMS.

*THEY WANT TO PUT LIMITS TO YOUR
IMAGINATION.
LITTLE THEY DO KNOW....
IT IS JUST THE BEGINNING OF YOUR RECREATION.
IT MIGHT SEEM THIS TIME AND THIS PROCESS ALL
OF THIS OPPOSES.
BUT REMEMBER...
YOU ARE THE PEARL FROM AN OYSTER.
YOU ARE THE DIAMOND IN THE HANDS OF A
MONISTER.
ONE DAY FOR SURE YOU WILL BE OUT OF THIS
CAGE.
AND ALL THIS WILL BE LIKE AN OLD TORN PAGE.
ALL THE STORMS WILL BE CALM MAY BE EVEN
SILENT .
AS YOU ARE GENIUS AND HIGHLY RESILENT .
YOU HAVE CREATED YOUR OWN PATH.
YOU ARE ALONE, BUT STILL FREE OF THEIR WRATH.
YOU ARE CREATIVE AND STRONG.
AND I KNOW ONE DAY YOU WILL PROVE ALL OF
THEM WRONG.*

3. BURNING ALLEY

The story of a valley.

The tale of a burning alley.

All the vultures and crows.

All the light fades and misery grows.

The snow and blood.

The fear and cold.

All of the power snatched.

All of the fighters encaptured.

The truth that beholds all lies.

And the courage that declines.

The crumbled heart of a mother.

The broken strenght of a father.

The tale of a widowed wife.

All her happiness gone and now only a miserable life.

A newborn unknown to her father.

And that man burried by the people together.

The orphans cry and wail.

Only injuries left and nothing to heal.

Crying for some miracle to happen.

But still all of the gallantary broken.

The confiscated words.

And the war of guns and swords.

Waiting for a day.....
A day full of gleam and light.
So that we could say "GOOD BYE" to this dark night.

4. A TALK WITH FEAR

THE FEAR TALKS TO ME OFTEN AND SOMETIMES
SEIZES MY SOUL.
THEN IT SAYS HEY! I AM HERE TO CRUMBLE THE
WHOLE.
IT SAYS "I WILL SUCK THE LIFE OUT OF YOU"
IT SAYS "I WILL SNATCH YOUR EVERY HUE"
IT SAYS "I WILL IMPRISON YOUR SPIRITS AND I WILL
TEAR YOU INTO BITS"
THE FEAR__ IT COMES TO ME AS A DARK NIGHT.
IT PUTS ME DOWN AND MAKES MY HEAD LIGHT.
THE FEAR__IT SAYS "I WILL SUCK EVERY TEAR OUT
OF YOU"
IT SAYS "I WILL DRINK EVERY DROP OF BLOOD
FROM YOU"
AH! IT SAYS__ "I WILL PUT YOU TO FAILURE"
IT SAYS "I AM THE ROAD AND YOU ARE THE
DRIVER"
OH! MY HEART,THIS FEAR IS LIKE A HOUND, IT
TREMBLES ME WITH
ITS SOUND.
THE FEAR__IT CONTINUES AND SAYS "I WILL DO
EVERYTHING,FOR I WANT TO TEST YOUR

COURAGE, AND I WANT TO MAKE YOU A SAVAGE"
THE FEAR__IT SAYS 'BUT STILL IF YOU PERSIST
THEN I WILL BECOME YOUR SHEILD'
IT SAYS "I WILL TRANSFORM MYSELF INTO
COURAGE AND I WILL LIE WITHIN YOU"
IT SAYS "I WILL STAY THERE TO GIVE YOU
STRENGTH AND I WILL RETURN YOUR HUE"
IT SAYS "IF YOU PERSIST I WILL GIVE YOU SPIRITS
TO SEE THE LIGHT, AND I WILL TAKE AWAY EVERY
DARK NIGHT"
THE FEAR SAYS "DEAR JUST TRY NOT TO BE AFRAID
OF ME, I AM HERE I WILL ALWAYS BE HERE,
BUT ONLY TRY TO HANDLE ME CAUTIOUSLY WITH
CARE"
IT SAYS "OH DEAR_WHEN YOU GET TO KNOW ME, I
WILL BECOME A MAGIC SPELL AND THEN YOU
WILL NEVER BE AFRAID AGAIN"

5. TO THAT LITTLE SCARED KID.

I know it is dark and gloomy.

I know it is dirty and shabby.

It might be tough and hard.

You might feel crazy and mad.

I know deeply what you feel.

Just beleive me you are about to heal.

Sometimes this darkness sinks your heart.

But to smile at it, it is your proactive art.

Your shevering nerves, and your trembling body.

But still you hold all of it with utmost audacity.

I know you are not fine but take my words ....

It is just matter of time.

I can feel the pounding of your heart.

I know when that teacher shouts at you.

I know how it feels when that stick hits you.

But that does't mean you need to shed your tears.

You don't need to give way to your fears,

One day you will grow...

And then all the misery will blow.

I know the feeling of being encaged in the prison of darkness.

I know that state of numbness.
I can feel the smell of your burning toys.
I can sense your head full of noise.
I can see at a young age your childhood and innocence were
burried.
I can see your burned face, crumbled heart and your soul
worried.
But still one day it will all be over.
And then you will be free of these fears forever.
One day you will come out shining so bright.
Smiling at your tears and laughing at your fears.

6. ROSE OF HEART

- *YOU SAY YOU ARE MERE AGONY OF MINE.*
- *I SAY IT IS ALL GOING TO BE FINE.*
- *I CRY AND SOMBER.*
- *YOU LAUGH AND WONDER.*
- *I THINK OF YOU AS A 'ROSE OF HEART''*
- *AND YOU REMEMBER ME AS THE 'SECRET OF LAKE'*
- *I TRY TO PERSIST, BUT YOU WANT ME TO FADE .*
- *OH DEAR! I WANT TO SAY I CAN'T RESIST BUT EVEN YOUR SOUL IS MADE*
- *WHENEVER I CRUMBLE I CLOSE MY EYES AND REMEMBER THE EVERY WORD YOU SAID EVERY TIME.*
- *AND EVEN WHEN THE DARKNESS WAS IN IT'S PRIME.*
- *WHEN FLOWERS WERE FROZEN AND MY WINGS WERE BROKEN.*
- *AND MY TEARS LIKE DEW DROPS ALL OVER.*
- *AND INFRONT OF MY EYES I SEE THAT BEAUTIFUL RIVER.*
- *IN WHOSE RHYTHM YOUR WORDS FLOW*

• *AND THAT IS WHAT MAKES MY HEART AGIN TO*
GLOW

7. TO ONLY YOU

Lost in the misery of hope.
Glitering away from the heavens .
This unnerving feeling often comes and trembles me.
Can't loose you amid stars.
Then I think "why not to become the blossom and wither away
with spring,
Rather than having longing in heart and yearning for you
forever"

8. A WOMAN...

She looks at him with the sweetest sight.
She thinks of him as a star which is so bright.
She left her joy and love of this world,
So that she can merge in his life.
But he never realised the sacrifice she always gave.
She gave him solace when he had lost his peace.
She gave him companionship when he was dwelling alone.
She gave his seed her blood to nurture.
And in return,
He broke her wings and scratched her soul with immense pain.
He gave her nothing but loneliness of dark nights.
He gave her painful heart and tearful eyes.
He crumbled her strenght and even burned her ashes...
He kept nothing in her sorrowful mind except those past
memories and promises...
All of what remained at last was...the incomplete story they had.
So then, she thought a little mourned over the pain he gave her
smiled over the smiles she gave him.
...On the edge of her life she was waiting for him to come and
embrace her
So all her pain could fade away.
But what she got was only a letter from him...

She had his love and longing
But she knew in real she was only his belonging.

9. DRABNESS IN A CLASSROOM

In this clasroom lies the encaged moon.
The demotivated students at corners.
And nothing like friends.
No curiosity for knowledge.
All they have is damage.
The enshackled mind.
And no one is kind.
The lost life and charm.
No strength and nothing is warm.
The mind and heart both apart.
The soul is sunken.
The tears dried up.
And the ears numb to the voices all along.
All of these people lack the love and strength to bear the
unknown.

10. DARKNESS

WHENEVER I LOOK UP TO MYSELF.
I FIND THOSE DARK SHADES.
ARE THOSE MY THOUGHTS.
OR JUST A HEART CRUMBLING NIGHTMARE.
IN THAT DARKNESS I AM SUPPOSED TO LIVE MY
LIFE
AS IN A CAGE.
WHENEVER I TRYTO TALK ABOUT IT.
THE IMAGE TURNS BLUR AND MY THOUGHTS
CEASE.
WHEN EVER I TRY TO EXPLAIN IT MY THROAT GETS
CHOCKED OUT
OF PAIN.
I NEVER HOLD BREATH TO TALK ABOUT THIS DARK
DREAM.
IT IS NOTHING BUT JUST MERE HELPESSNESS OF
MINE...
IT IS A QUESTION OF TIME.
BUT IT HAS A CURE WITH IT.
IT WILL BE OVER SOON .
AND THEN I WILL BE FREE FOREVER.

11. A BEAUTIFUL THOUGHT

I WILL GLEAM WITH YOU IN MORNING SHINE.

I WILL RISE WITH YOU IN EVENING PRIME.

YET IF YOU ARE NOT ABLE TO HOLD ME.

THEN COME AND JUST TELL IT TO ME.

I AM LIKE A BEAM OF SUNLIGHT.

I AM ALWAYS FULL OF DELIGHT.

I DON'T GIVE WAY TO AGONY.

AND YOU DON'T NEED TO CARE ABOUT MY MISERY.

I AM WHOLE OF UNIVERSE WITHIN ME.

I AM COURAGEOUS AND CALM, I HOLD HAPPINESS WITHIN ME.

I AM THOUGHT OF A MORNING ANGEL.

I AM AS BEAUTIFUL AS BRIDES BANGEL.

I AM WAY TOO BOLD AND STRONG.

I AM BRAVE AND I ACCEPT NOTHING WRONG.

12. MERE STATE OF HELPLESSNESS

This imagination, and i have lost my concentration.
This hallucination,they have lost their consideration.
This time is tersely.
And my heart is now a misery.
Oh! this oblivion…none of my opinion.
Their time is lucrative, and my mind is no more creative.
All of this indispensable, my souls feels incapable.
Oh! Baby let me tell you 'you are the morning sunshine'
And this all is not your decline.
You don't need to be crying all day.
You don't need to regret the burning hay.
Let me tell you 'you are the soul of fire'
You are the breeze and air.
You are the crystal in this coal mine.
You are the diamond,strong and fine.
Let me tell you 'I would like to let you free'
You are pure just like the blossom from heaven's tree.
I would like to cherish you.
I would like to love you.
You are an ocean of wisdom.

Few drops of tears, and you can create the whole kingdom.

13. STORY FROM A DARK EVENING

- *you write words.*
- *i imagine herds.*
- *you try to explain.*
- *but ah! I just strain.*
- *you try to comprehend.*
- *i let it end up.*
- *this chalk and marker.*
- *but my mind a hacker.*
- *trying to write it.*
- *but just to imitate.*
- *carrying the burden.*
- *shame and guilt burried in bosom of this garden.*
- *all of you acting as mentors .*
- *still all of us standing as warriors.*
- *the door is smashed.*
- *and our dignity feels abashed.*
- *my heart is pounding.*
- *my mind is racing.*
- *the thoughts are frozen.*

- *and my courage broken.*
- *trying to stand up,*
- *asking to wind up,*
- *but now this soul is scratched.*
- *and my spirits detached.*
- *tears dry up.*
- *still trying to rise up.*
- *but feeling helpless.*
- *all of you acting as mentors, just to satisfy your own concerns.*
- *that trauma seizes my breath.*
- *it plunges me to death.*
- *but still I know we all need to fight it.*
- *may be it is not so straight.*
- *but we ought to have our strength.*

14. GLOMMY PEOPLE

THAT DARK ALLEY AND MY SHEVERING NERVES.
MY HELPLESS FRIENDS AND ME SWERVES.
YOU ARE SAYING THE WORDS ON THAT UPLIFTED
STAGE.
YOU ARE WRITING YOUR OPINION ON A
CRUMBLED PAGE.
YOU ARE SHOWING THE POWER WHICH IS JUST
NULL.
YOUR ARE SMASHING YOUR OWN SKULL.
YOU ARE WRITING A STORY WHICH HAS ITS
BEGNING AS END.
YOU ARE FLOWING IN A RIVER WHICH HAS NO
BEND.
YOU ARE CALLING ME THE INCAPABLE AND MAYBE
PROBLEMATIC.
BUT NOW THIS IS ENOUGH...YOU ARE BEING
TRAUMATIC.

15. OBLIVION

I WANT THIS TIME TO FINISH.
I WANT THIS MISERY TO VANISH.
I WANT THIS LOVE TO LAST.
I WANT TO COME OUT OF PAST.
I WANT TO GET UP AND GLOW.
I WANT TO OPPOSE THE FLOW.
I FEEL LIKE...
A WRITER IN A CAGED RING.
A FIGHTER WITH A BROKEN WING.
A CLOUD WITH A GLITTERING END.
AND A SWORD WITH A GOLDEN BEND
A THOUGHT IN A JUVENILE MIND.
I WANT TO BE...
A WARRIOR IN THE BATTLEFIELD.
A FARMER WITH A HIGH YEILD .
A TEACHER WITH IMMENSE EMPATHY.
A DOCTOR FULL OF SYMPATHY.
AN ARTIST WITH UTMOST CREATIVITY.
A MOTHER WITH DEEP SERENITY.
ALL OF IT I KNOW.
IS ME JUST LIKE SNOW.
MELTING WITH THE GRACE.

DANCING IN THE RACE.
FALLING FROM THE HEIGHT.
YET FULL OF LIFE AND DELIGHT.

• 25 •

16. POEM OF LOVE

THE BEARER OF ALL THE WORLDS.
I BEG TO YOU FOR EVERLASTING PEACE.
I ASK TO YOU FOR THE HEALING OF MY SOUL.
I ASK TO YOU FOR THE REPAIRMENT OF MY HEART,
YOU ARE THE GREAT AND GREATEST OF ALL.
YOU ARE THE STRONGEST AND MERCIFUL OF ALL.
YOU ARE KIND AND DIVINE.
YOU ARE LOVE AND LIGHT BOTH COMBINE.
YOU ARE ALL ALONE INCREDIBLE.
YOU ARE THE GITA, QURAN AND THE BIBLE.
THEN LET NOT MY LOVE BLEED TO WOUNDS.
AND SCUMB ME TO DEATH.
LET IT BE THE POWER TO HEAL MY SOUL.
AND MY HEART MY BODY AS WHOLE.
LET IT BE THE ZEST IN MY LIFE.
LET IT BE A BLESSING TO MY HEART AND SOUL.

17. THE PERFECT ILLUSION

if i let you loose your colour.

i know it will also make me duller.

you are a transparent glass in your thoughts.

and that red dark wine in your emotions.

to me you don't just come as a mere thought.

to me you bloom like an evening primrose.

you fight through out the day and night.

i keep singing for your joy and delight.

i am bearer of all the pain.

but now it feels it is all in vain.

you leave along the lines of stars.

i wander along the sea shores.

you keep going to that wonderland.

and i keep listening to that same old band.

it feels as if love falls apart.

and the love and the lover depart.

it may even feel like a shooting star.

it also feels like distance not so far.

it feels the time in illusion.

it feels like the thoughts in delusion.

18. THE SUN

SUNRISES AND SHINES,
IT GLEAMS AND GLOWS.
OVER THE SKY IT BURNS.
BUT STILL BENEATH IT EVERYTHING WORKS.
IT NOURISHES AND CHERISHES EVERY SOUL.
IT BRINGS WITH IT HAPPINESS AS A WHOLE.
THE SUNSETS AND RISES AGAIN,
ONCE AGAIN IT BRINGS JOY TO WORD...
ONCE AGAIN IT BURNS LIKE THE OLD.
IT GIVES SUNSHINE TO YOUR WORLD AND MINE
TOO.
IT BRINGS DARKNESS TO END.
AND DOES'T SHOW ANY BEND
IT PERSISTS AND WORKS.
IT SHOWS DETERMINATION AND GLOWS.

19. VIRTUE OF COURAGE

YOU DON'T LET THE PAIN TO PLUNGE IN.
YOU DON'T LET THE MISERY TO GLOW IN.
YOU ARE A STRONG MOUTAIN.
YOU ARE TALL AND FIRM.
I AM LOST PETAL OF ROSE
AND AS DELICATE AS DUSK.
I AM THE BLUR IMAGE OF THE TWILIGHT.
I AM CALMNESS OF THE MORNING SUN.
I MAYBE THUNDER OF A STORMY NIGHT.
I AM WANDERING IN THE CAGE OF YOUR
THOUGHTS.
I FEEL TO FLEE WITH YOUR MERE SMILE.
I LIVE NOT FOR A DAY OUT.
I AM HERE TO LET ME BREATH OF LIGHT.
I KNOW THIS PAIN IS SO ROUGH.
AND THESE LESSONS QUIT TOUGH.
I WANT YOU TO CONTEMPLATE THESE THOUGHTS.
I DON'T WANT YOUR SWORDS.

20. THE SIGHT OF FIRST LOVE

She froze, and He vanished.
Quick was the sight of love.
The eyes met and the tears shed.
She was cold like an iceberg.
and he was fierce like sunlight.
Both felt apart.
I think this love was only to depart.
She cried in deep pain.
Trying to hide every scar.
The naive heart has its reasons for sure.
But these feelings they are too pure.
Was this inner call or just a war.
After all, the first love is sweet and sour.
All those beautiful moments and memories!
How can they crumble heart and become now worries.

21. WHEN YOU ARE ILL

WHEN YOU ARE ILL.
AND YOU HAVE THAT BROKEN WILL.
WHEN ANXIETY TRIGGERS.
AND BLOOD RUSHES.
AND THE LUNGS ARE CHOCKED.
AND THE BREATH IS SEIZED.
ALL I KNOW IS…IT HURTS.
IT HURTS A LOT AND A LOT.
WHEN YOU CAN'T BREATH.
WHEN YOU CAN'T EAT.
STILL THE STRENGTII MATTERS.
TO DEAL WITH IT YOU NEED TO SHOW, LITTLE BIT
OF RESILIENCE.
JUST REMEMBER…
THE PAIN WILL FADE AWAY QUICKLY.
YOU WILL BE REBORN NEW AND LIVELY.
AND THEN YOU WILL CHEERUP HAPPILY

22. WHEN I LOST HIM

Looking at these lights.
It reminds me of his beautiful sights.
The tears he never let me shed.
And all the kisses on my forehead.
He held me high in his dreams and words.
We were in love like the love birds.
The morning thought he was for me.
And the precious pearl of my love he will always be.
This darkness is full of drabness.
And our love full of incompleteness.
But my heart enlightned by his name.
All of my love questions me along.
And our incomplete love song.
Telling me...
"not to your heart he ever belonged
but your love has still prolonged"

23. IF YOU ARE MY BESTFRIEND.

If you are my bestfriend,
Then beleive me I will never let this story end.
I know this castle of emotions is made of sand.
But my heart will have all your pure and pious land.
If you are my bestfriend,
I will stay by your side.
I will take you with me in memories worldwide.
If you are my bestfriend,
I will trust you to the all my strength.
And I will compress all the distance.
If you are my bestfriend,
And you ever try to leave me.
I will let you go, but never from my heart.
Maybe you will think better thoughts without me.
And a better life all alone.
If you are my bestfriend,
I will let light to emerge in for the better sight and seen.
If you are my bestfriend,
I will never lie to you
I will never hide anything from you.

If you are my bestfriend,
I will let you be in your own colours.
I will let you enjoy all the hours.
DEAR BESTFRIEND...
When you will grow and glow.
When you will sheen and shine.
May be you might remember.
That you had a bestfriend too.
Because with time all friends are lost .
But the true ones stay same and stay forever.

24. LIBERATED AND FREE

*AND YOUR IMAGINATION WILL BE CLEAR AND
WIDE.*

25. THE TRUTH OF LIFE

A prison is the one in mind.
A prison is nothing of shackles, but everything unkind.
A prison is the loss of faith.
Encaptured mind and soul aftermath.
The soul that sinks deep into the ink of darkness.
The mind that tries to liberate from the thoughts of lifelessness.
All these together create the way for improvements.
All these together grow into little achivements.
Sometimes heart pounds for sure.
And those tears come down rolling which are mere.
But it doesn't mean you loose the sight within.
It signifies the intensity of rays of light that are getting in.
The process is tough and hard.
This journey might be rough and bad.
May be it makes you cry.
May be you want now to sigh.
But this is life and it demands to be tough.
This is the strength of light and it will be rough.
To get fulgent gleam of sun.
You need to burn with firece heat and run.

26. I AM WAITING FOR THE DAY TO COME

I am waiting for a day to come.
When you will stay by my side.
Holding my hands and telling me your stories.
I am waiting for a day to come.
When you will look into my eyes, the way
you looked at your loved one.
One day I might perish from the sight of this world.
But my soul It will only sing your songs as whole.
It will think of your charam and love.
It think of the pain I owe.
I am waiting for the day to come.
when we will talk of the tales the world had ever so.
and we will talk about all the theories you know.
I am waiting for the day to come
when you will come back home to me.
when you will sing the songs of consciousness with me.
I am waiting for the day to come.
To keep your smile as a gift of patience for me
and as a token of reverence for my fragile heart.

I AM WAITING FOR YOU TO COME.
TO COME AND STAY WITH ME FOREVER.

27. STORY OF MOON

I know this moon has a story.

I know it has a tale it never revealed to anybody.

Once upon a time she felt in love with a star.

Whole of the universe knew it was bizzare.

But for love, it is naive and natural.

With the estactic elements she grew fond of him.

The supreme sun played with the gleam of moon.

But moon kept fading in the brightness of the sun.

She turned invisible and lost her sight.

Impalpable always she was, she was tortured and became blind.

Now came the time to seperate.

That is when pain felt even more.

Her shining bright body.

And the star also had supreme audacity.

All of the oblivion came into play.

Now the question was what she will rely on.

All her charm and light gone.

But she choose a diffrent path.

She went into the darkness to save the little ,

gleam, she was left with.

But all the scars still remained visible.

Even in that far sky they enlightned.

She had no shame for those battle scars.
Because they were from the fight with life
and all the wars.
She kept all her marks preserved to be observed
eveynight, when she was out with stars to shine bright.

28. dark magic

The girl I knew was strong and bold.
Then she met a woman fragile and old.
The story brgun...
Wome came up the tale of sand.
She was beautiful with a magical hand.
The girl swayed for a minute.
And she danced for infinite.
She had some magic done on her.
She had her wings and never let her run.
She slayed her with muscial tone.
She made her hallucinate and broke her strength and bone.
The women had power of infinite Magic.
And the girl was now all tragic.
All her beauty was sunken .
All her tears now an ocean.
She lost her soul and peace.
She lost her heart and heartsease.
Never came she out of that illusion.
Never finished that confusion.
She tried hard everyday to become better.
But it always felt like a cruel cold winter.

29. JOURNEY

SINKING INTO THE HOLE OF DESPAIR AND MISERY.
I LOST THE COURAGE AND GALLANTRY.
THE DARKNESS AND DUMBNESS OF FEAR.
THE COLDNESS AND AGONY OF THIS YEAR.
IT TOOK SEVERAL THINGS FAR FROM ME.
IT TOOK LIGHT AND LIFE AWAY FROM ME.
BUT STILL FIGHTING THIS WAR WILL BE AN
HONOR.
FIGHTING ALL THE COLD, DARKNESS AND
INCAPABILITY.
IT WILL ALL BE A BRAVERY.
SOMETIMES MY HEART WANTS TO LEAVE,
EVERYTHING AMID AND RUN.
BUT I KNOW IF I DON'T FIGHT IT WILL BE NO FUN.
ONLY THIS PART OF JOURNEY IS NOT ROUGH...
BUT WHOLE OF THE JOURNEY AND THIS PROCESS
IS TOUGH.
THEN COME AND FIGHT IT....
WITH THE STRENGTH AND STRONG WILL.
EVEN IF YOU LOOSE YOU WILL BE NOT A FAILURE.

30. LOVE AND DESIRE

You want me to wait for you.
But I know you won't talk to me.
Your empty words express love to me.
But it is pure toxicity.
You talk to me in a sober way.
But deep down your heart there is no love left for me.
AND I...
I am broken and perished.
Like the lit candle.
I am nothing but melted soul.
Like a murdered heart.
Well, my tears don't mean anything to you.
For you, your own spirits and joy matters.
I think every creature who loves, loves for their own joy.
For the hormonal rush they have.
For the dose of oxytocin and may be more.
Never think someone loves you for yourself.
Heart is naive but desires never are.
The love and lust are only words apart in todays world.
All we find is desires in the name of untrue love.
There is nothing like love they say.
If it is then why do the possesssion exists.

Why does hatred not fade.
And why does pure hearts crumble.
And why does love not become the cure for chastity.

• 45 •

31. FIERCE

I CAN'T BELEIVE CAN A WOMEN STILL LOVE A MAN.
A MAN WHO BROKE HER INTO BITS.
A MAN WHO CURSES HER DAILY AND HITS HER
BADLY.
HOW CAN SHE LOVE A MONSTER.
HOW CAN SHE NOT BECOME A FIGHTER.
WHY DOES SHE STILL BELEIVE HIM.
WHY CAN'T SHE LEAVE HIM.
THE MAN SHE LOVED WAS NEVER INNOCENT.
SHE KNEW EVERYTHING AND EVEN TRIED TO BE
VALYANT.
BUT IT SCRATCHED HER SOUL.
RUINED HER BEAUTY AS WHOLE.
SHE WAS A BROKEN BRANCH FROM THE TREE OF
COURAGE.
AND A CRUMBLED ROSE FROM THE BUSH OF
GALLANTARY.
WHEN WILL SHE RISE AGAIN TO ROAR…NO ONE
KNOWS.
BUT HER PAIN IS DEEPLY IMMERSED IN HER SOUL.
SHE WANTS ANSWERS TO MILLIONS OF QUESTIONS.

*SHE WANTS THE CURE OF ALL THE MOMENTS
SPEND WITH HIM.
SHE WANTS HER DIGNITY GRACE AND CHARM.
SHE WANTS HER NATURE WHICH WAS FIERCE AND
WARM.*

32. SOMEDAY

SOMEDAY WHEN YOU WILL FALL IN LOVE,
YOU WILL KNOW THE REASON OF MY MADNESS.
SOMEDAY WHEN YOUR HEART WILL BEAT FOR
SOMEONE,
YOU WILL KNOW THE REASON OF MY SADNESS.
SOMEDAY WHEN YOU WILL LOOSE THE LOVE OF
YOUR
LIFE, YOU WILL KNOW THE PAIN I SUFFERED.
SOMEDAY WHEN SHE WILL LEAVE YOU,
YOU WILL REALISE MY PAIN ENCAPTURED.
FOR NOW YOUR CONSCIOUSNESS IS INACTIVE.
FOR NOW YOU SEE WORLD ONLY IN YOURSELF.
BUT BELEIVE ME WHEN YOU WILL FALL IN LOVE
AND BREAK.
YOU WILL REALISE THE WAY I LOVED YOU.
YOU WILL REALISE WHY I HAD TO DIE A LIVING
DEATH.
BECAUSE FOR LOVE, IT TRAPS YOUR SOUL.
IT BINDS YOUR HEART TO UNKNOWN.
IT RESOLVES AND RESEMBLES
ALL THE FACTS OF YOUR EXISTENCE.
IT TAKES YOU TO CONTINUITY.

AND THE OCEAN OF PERSISTENCE.
IT MAKES YOU A DWELLER LIKE THE
AUTUMN LEAVES.
IT BURNS YOU WITH ALL FLAMES.
IT PLAYS IN YOU HUNDREDS OF GAMES.
AND AT LAST...
IT DECEIVES YOU OF YOUR EXISTENCE.
IT MAKES YOU A MERE THOUGHT.
IT GIVES NOTHING BUT PAIN AND LONGING.

33. IT IS ALL LIFE

When you say I want some courage.
When you say I have all the damage.
When you want to create your portrayal.
And then you again remember that betrayal.
The times when you felt apart.
The times when you felt your soul wants to depart.
The times when your throat was chocked.
The times when your consciousness was shocked.
Then you realised this world is unpredictable.
Then you realised it is not convincible.
The facts of reality can ruin the naive heart.
And this life it can smear the colours into incredible art.
When you realise this world is cruel.
And then you realise this world is calm too.
All of your facts depend on the vision you have.
All of your life is the attitude you possess.
With time you realise struggle teaches you strength.
With time you realise panic teaches you utmost calmness.
With time you realise pain gives you full growth.
With time you realise death gives you elixir of life.
IT IS ALL LIFE....
It trumbles you only to teach you unknown and inevitable.

It is life it enshackles you to teach the art of freedom.
It is life it punches you to build the firmness in you.
Because it is life it tests your brains, blood and muscle.
The reality of life is tough and hard.
The truth of life is quit and broad.
Life pushes you hard until you are know to yourself.
It smashes you bad untill you are revealed to your purpose

34. THE SUN

SUNRISES AND SHINES, IT GLEAMS AND GLOWS.
OVER THE SKY, IT BURNS.
BUT STILL, BENEATH IT EVERYTHING WORKS.
IT NOURISHES AND CHERISHES EVERY SOUL.
IT BRINGS WITH IT HAPPINESS AS A WHOLE.
THE SUNSETS AND RISES AGAIN.
ONCE AGAIN IT BRINGS JOY TO THE WORLD.
ONCE AGAIN IT BURNS LIKE THE OLD.
IT GIVES THE SUNSHINE TO YOUR WORLD AND
MINE TOO.
IT BRINGS THE DARKNESS TO END.
AND STILL IT DOESN'T SHOW ANY BEND.
IT PERSISTS AND WORKS.
IT SHOWS DETERMINATION AND GLOWS.

35. STRUGGLING SOULS IN A CAGE

AH! This cage.
And my rage.
Want to destroy them, of my wrath.
But I know that is never the right path.
I may be evil.
They are no less devil.
There taunts, it just haunts.
The way they shout,
I just blacked out.
All of it a misery,
I just feel crazy, may be not surely.
Physcis formulas and chemical reactions.
All of them oblivion none of the actions.
"Biological processes" Ah! Misery enhances .
The struggle of the Oxygen.
And the fight of the Antigen.
Submission to the gravity.
Obsession to the clarity.
Misery of the magnetism.
And fairy tales of catabolism.

The story of the solenoid.
And order of the structures with the void.
Genes in the genetics.
The heridity fragments.
Physcis says...
The centre of mass
And chemistry repeats the history of copper and brass.
Charge with frequency.
And the current with intensity.
All of this dumbness in the dark.
And now our teacher talking about something called
electric arc.
This story of endless events.
And the struggle with immense efforts

36. THE QUEEN SHE WAS!

A fairytale emerged in a wonderland.
But that castle was only made of sand.
That queen had no crown.
Neither the land was her own.
A place faraway in the dark woods.
Then she came fighting all the odds.
A Princess being a fighter .
Autumn becoming the winter.
Her golden soft hands.
And her silver broken shackles.
All the strength she had.
And all those colours that fade.
Shattering into pieces.
And the strength she releases.
Misery into the dark night.
But she has the intensity of the sunlight.
She gets up every morning.
With full gleam she is swarming.
The ghosts around,
And darkness bound,

She still manages to cut the veil.
She is out there to heal.
All of a sudden she trembles and falls.
But still she learned to love her flaws.

37. CALLING

because life is calling.
then cheer up darling.
stay calm and give some love to yourself.
you are pretty and cute.
you don't need to stay mute.
just be "you" and show this world your hue.
you don't need to change.
just stick to your image.
because they all are saying, still it is not your damage.
it is the fall before the rise.
it is all the charm in your beautiful eyes

38. BROKEN HER...

Love was never my word.
May be for me it was abhorred.
Because I knew a girl.
And the ashes of her soul burned.
All the charm she had.
All those colours fade.
That fairytale she will never owe.
And her dying love.
Her fragile mourning heart.
She knew that story will never restart.
I heard....
She wanted him not to go far away.
She wanted him just to stay.
But she knew it...whenever she falls in love,
It is pure and intense.
She knew it is fragile and unfaithful.
Everytime she felt love deep inside chambers of her heart.
It came out to be a great blunder.
Everytime she trusted someone it was only one third.
Because she knew her love was only the spirit.
She knew it was ecstatic.
But for the world it was the tale of two.

May be red,purple,green,black or blue.
But for her it was the reality of unknown.
Not a mere muscial tone.
She knew her energy in the motion.
She felt joy at his mere presence.
She knew it was love with the pure essence.
But she never reacted nor did she reply.
Because she knew it...it will be another heartbreak .
Or may be a blunder gain.
But still she felt in love, without him knowing her.....

39. DEAR DAUGHTER.

I WANT TO WRITE TO YOU, FEW LETTERS.
I WANT TO TELL YOU THE TALES OF ALL THE
WORLDS.
I WANT FOR YOU THE LOVE OF LOTUS FLOWERS.
I WANT FOR YOUR LIFE THE PURENESS OF
MORNING DEW DROPS.
THE CALMNESS OF THE BEACH.
AND THE TOP MOST HEIGHTS I WANT YOU TO
REACH.
MY DEAR DAUGHTER!
I WANT YOU TO BE FREE OF FEAR.
YOU DON'T NEED TO MAKE ME PROUD BY
SACRIFICING YOUR DREAMS.
YOU DON'T NEED TO LIE TO ME IN ANY TERMS.
I WANT YOU TO BE HAPPY AND STRONG.
I WANT YOU TO BE ENOUGH BOLD SO YOU COULD
SAY "NO" TO WRONG.
I WANT YOU TO GIVE WAY TO EMOTIONS.
BUT I DON'T WANT YOU TO BE AN EMOTIONAL
FOOL.
I DO WANT YOU TO LOVE EVERYONE.
BUT I DON'T WANT LOVE TO BREAK YOU.

DEAR DAUGHTER!
YOU ARE THE BEAUTY MY LIFE HAS GOT.
YOU ARE THE VICTORY OF MY WAR,
THEN HOW COME I WILL EVER WANT SOMEONE TO
RUIN THE STRONG TREE OF YOUR EMOTIONS.
I WANT YOU TO BE RESILENT TO THE THROWS
AND THORNS OF LIFE.
BUT REMEMBER YOU CAN COME TO ME ALWAYS...
BECAUSE I AM YOUR MOTHER.
YOU CAN SPILL ALL YOUR EMOTIONS.
AND BELEIVE ME YOU WON'T BE JUDGED.
BECAUSE FOR ME YOU ARE, "MY DAUGHTER"
THE ROSE OF MY THORNY GARDEN.
AND A DIAMOND OF MY COAL MINE.
YOU ARE THE EPITOME OF ALL MY HAPPINESS.
AND YOU ARE MY GREATEST BLESSING.

40. MOTHER

The pearl of love and music of heart.
All together come and sway on the bay.
And tears roll down like stones of a bold
moutain.
Sometimes I never am able to conclude
Myself in simple words.
Flames burn in the names of many.
But her sight is sweet for me and the
memories are just like honey.
She is the sight of morning sunshine.
She is the beauty and my lifeline.
The creature created out of love.
The strength and depth all her qualities.
The angelic beauty and the soft spoken
words.
All her elegance deep and serene.

41. lost lover

The love that fades away from me.
And my soul with a question alone...
Recalls the beauty his words had...
And my name with a sparkless shine.
Left me in my impriosned smile.
The talk we had....full of frost.
And my tears like summer rain.
In the corner of my heart dark shadow resides.
In my eyes I possess a glittery charm of him.
Blurred but still beat of my heart.
Warmth of the fever, I had the night when he
left me...still possess my mind.

42. OH! DEAR BREATH.

Wither away from me...OH! Dear breath.
Let me hold up the life of death.
I mourn for the joy this world gives me...
And deep down my heart, I love the pain you gift me.
Oh! Dear Breath, you are the honey of my heart.
Let this death take me away and plunge me in a
dreamless sleep.
I know it will be full of heartsease.
And my mind also wants some peace.
I know I will yen for you and cry.
But then every ail will fade out,
Leaving me solely in my own world.
It will be time when you will leave me...OH! DEAR BREATH.
I will be dead but surviving my death to utmost,
and smiling at my heart.
Then time will pass...
My body will decay, my name and frame will
vanish away from the sight of the world.
Merely my heart, it will crumble and break.
My mind it will be full of inutility.

But it will be only my soul full of words
on that night.
On the edge of my life...
It will speak of the dreams I had ever so.

43. FREEDOM FOR ME.

Just like a dew driblet at the betimes of day.
I keep on craving and keep on begging for
some heartsease.
Simply never more my heart replies!
But always rely on the fact that I am through
with my life.
Oh! Stars speak to me, I lack fulgent gleam
of yours.
Talk to me I want to sheen of yours.
I want a day full of dreams and night
without darknessnd.
And a sight full of shine
I want this sun and sky to be mine.
Lost in my own shadow...
Can't upkeep why not to laugh.
I want hue of my life that is deep and dark.
I draw a bead on to breath with you.
That life is my,
And I want to colour it with the colours
that existed never before...

It is freedom for me...
It is freedom for me...

44. FACTS OF THE LIFE

One day I was thinking in a dreamless night.
My dreams were blurr and I had no sight.
I was just thinking of the orange flowers
which I love.
There are many of them but to me roses are the one.
I love the petals and leaves equally.
I love the thorns and dew drops explicitly.
For me dreams and realities are inevitable.
I think of some people whom I left far away.
I think of dreams which are shattered.
I recall certain things and the beauty of
certain days.
I think of sunshine and sunset.
I think of stars and moonlight.
All I conclude is the efforts required to live
the life are delicate and strong.

45. INTROSPECTION

Sometimes my mind skips a few words.
Sometimes my thoughts cling to some odds.
Sometimes I become tough and rigid.
Sometimes my thoughts are switched.
Then I think of this life, love and light.
Then I feel I need to fight...
I feel I need to fight my own thoughts,
Without any guns and swords.
The bizzare story of the mind.
And my gleam which I want to find.
I wonder sometimes, will it be easy.
Or will it make me crazy,
But still, It is the story of will and chase.
There is nothing easy and nothing full of
ease.
It is the story of the power over love.
It is the strength which I need to owe.
It is all truth bound to fake lies.
It is the blood of all relations and deep ties.
It is the tale my mother narrated to me.
It is the story my father often told me.
To let grow your will strong and sufficient.

And to make yourself more efficient.
You need to develop a few magical qualities.
You need to nourish a few of your ablities.
Worry not! only come out of that comfort
zone.
Come to the real world and listen to its beautiful
tone.
Fight the odds...
I am sure you will have your own struggles.
Defying your incapabilities .
You will develop your greatest abilities.
A fighter doesn't fight the world alone.
But for her it starts from within...maybe from
her own bone.
Somtimes life wants a few more dew drops.
Sometimes more sunshine is needed to grow
beautiful crops.
We need efforts to develop srong
foundations.
And sometimes we need blood and tears
to create strong emotions.

46. MY SUPER TEACHER.

In my vivid imagination there used to be a teacher.
And for me he had always been a legendary creature.
He was a great influential personality.
And also had the presence of emotionality.
For his students he was honest and encouraging.
And he dealt with every bit that was challenging.
He enlightened my life with his knowledge,
And brought my thoughts from darkness to
sheen of stars.
He pacified me and motivated me when I was full of fear.
I don't knew who was he, and even I never found him in
reality.
In my imagination he had created a space.
He brought me to heartsease when there
was no were peace.
He was my super teacher and was full of
inspiring qualities.
With time I grew up and don't got any
teacher to fit in the frame of my super
teacher.

And then one day I entered a classroom.
My eyes got sight of a person writing on the white
board.
And my frame of SUPER TEACHER was filled up
by a picture.
The teacher I found writing there was a man of great name.
He had gleam of knowledge in his eyes
And sheen of depth in his thoughts.
His words explained realites of life.
He had a deep bond of kindness with his students.
And he worked hard for there improvements.
He was a mindful person with a kindful heart.
He was full of experience and had travelled thousand journeys
I was full of rejoice when I started to recognise,
The frame my imagination had framed, of my
super teacher had a name written on it...
He possessed every quality of my super teacher.
And yes, He is for me a great leader

47. INSOMNIA...

My eyes are open wide.
And this pain can't be hide.
My soft spoken words often quarrel
with my mind.
And my heart tries to get peace which i can't find.
Oh! Is this a mere apperance of me which keeps
me alive.
Or it is a thought of thoughtlessness which
puts me in a hive.
These winds are becoming strong storms.
They have hault me and chained my arms.
My breath has been seized and even my ashes burnt.
My mind has been put in a cage and my words impriosned.
I have been put in a dark dream and my senses are
totally lost.
NO,NO,NO,
I am not dead but even not alive.
I am living this life with purposeless aim.
My shadow is gone and my traces are no were left.
My voice is frozen and my throat is silt.
The sun has suck all my blood and left me
helpless.

And this night is killing me of its darkness.
My sleep is vanished.
And my thoughts are wandering.
This hijacked mind and the numb body.
All my imagination is dark and spotty.

48. Within

The name that is written with dark ink.
And my eyes they can't blink.
Sometimes the defeat gives us the courage to see the world.
And sometimes world defeats us to see within.
Within are the elements of the power and strength.
Within are the elements of deafeat and helplessness.
To see the world with gleam is the song of gallantary.
To live life with honor is the utmost bravery.
Within lies the answer of all the questions.
Within lies the strength to bear all the difficulties.
There is no limit of time to acheive things.
Because within lies the strength to hold yourself.
All the difficulties and adversities have solutions within.
Every crumbled heart heals within.
And every scratched soul nourishes within.

49. SHADOW OF THE UNKNOWN

If he is my shadow, then why can't he gleam
in my joy.
He touches every height of the pain.
And gives me the feeling of his feelinglessness.
He tries to give my life the poison of his words.
He tries so hard, but still it is not worthwhile.
He tries every minute not to love me.
but still he is meek.
He has my smile encaptured in his name.
He has my tears imprisoned in his thoughts.
And what more can he possess of mine
That dark khol of my eyes which he
remembers day and night.
I know it is not my beauty which has trapped
his heart.
But these are my words which have imprisoned
his soul long ago.
He will never end to love me...even after
forgetting my name.
He will still be remembering the glimpse

of mine.
He will still be confused about my shadow and sheen.
But still I can't label him mean.

50. INSECTA

Insects are the minature toys of nature.
They have sheen to gleam the world.
They have a story just like a locked treasure.
I call up the beauty all those insects had.
When I used to be in the garden along with my dad.
I have seen some snails.
I used to prick up them with my nails.
Oh! I don't know what to say about ants.
When I was a toddler they creeped up my pants.
I love some inscets like moths and butterflies.
But I have an indiffrence towards the eyes of dragonflies.
When I look at the bees they have many species.
Honey bees, Bumble bees they have a habitat to live in colonies.
With earthworms I used to play dissection game.
I usually talk of spiders.
i don't know why?
But to me they are like armed soliders.
At the bee times of the day I see some of them.
They have thousands secrets which are unrevealed
to the world.
They fly and they swim they creep and they crawl.
All the creatures are heaven created.

But insects have been abundantly generated.

51. OH! People

For sure you can't conclude me in your words.
But for me measures exist even in my dreams.
Being at the back doesn't show my dumbness.
But indicates the wound that has put me back.
I want to abstain from the sight of world.
But in my mind I can't resist all this
trembling effect.
"No" I say to this world.
Don't hide up this fact.
My life is like an iceberg.
And I am melting like frozen ice.
This world is full of history.
And every creature has its story.
Colours can't be blend with dark shades.
And peace can't be get through silence.
When you speak of yourself then try to be free.
When you express yor thoughts then let
your mind be glee.
The darkness may imprison several thoughts.
But what about the thoughts which get
imprisoned in the cell of darkness.
Your dreams may give you supplement to

live the life.
But what about the life which gives way to
these dreams.
An empty mind can't create thoughts out
of pessimism.
And a well enscripted mind brings
everything out of optimism.
A painful heart can't deal with emotions.
And a happy heart brings everything to charm.
This world might try to give you its colour.
But try your best to be it's creative artist.

52. emotions and sensations

SOMETIMES MY HEART TRAVELLES MILES.
AND MY MIND GOES UP THROUGH THE SKIES.
A POET CAN EXPRESS MORE THAN HER WORDS.
BUT THIS WORLD WANTS PEACE ONLY THROUGH
SWORDS.
EMOTIONS ARE NEVER TO BE BURRIED.
EMOTIONS ARE BONE TO WORRIED.
HEAVENS CAN'T MAKE A SMILE GREATER THAN
HER.
AND MY THOUGHTS THEY ARE BURNING LIKE FUR.
A RAINDROP CAN'T BECOME TEAR OF EYE.
AND STARS CAN'T SAY BYE TO SKY.
THE RULES OF LIFE ARE JUST LIKE FIRE.
THEY CAN NEVER BURN THE AIR.
MY LIFE IS WRITTEN ON BLANK PAGES.
AND IT WILL TAKE HIM LONG TO READ THESE
IMAGES.
SOMTIMES AUTUMNN WINDS TRY TO EVADE
THE BEAUTY OF FLOWERS.
AND SOMETIMES BLOSSOMS BECOME JUST

LIKE DWELLERS.
SOMETIMES A DEEP THOUGHT FLASHES
ACROSS MY MIND.
WHY IS IT THAT NATURE IS SO PURE AND KIND.

53. THE LOSS

When you loose yourself amid stars.
When you find yourself amid scars.
Your days and nights gone only to darkness.
Your fights and struggles with helplesness.
Then why don't you get up and gather your courage.
Then why don't you wakeup and resolve your damage.
Crying day and night won't yeild anything.
Pain and misery should not become everything.
Get up and glow.
All the misery will blow.
This time might be not so good.
But you ought to work on you and
you definitely should.
When life has given you chance.
Then you need your happiness to enhances.

54. FAITH

THE COLOURS THAT SPLASH.
AND THE THOUGHTS THAT CRASH.
YOU MIGHT HAVE CREATED A PLAN.
BUT GOD WILL NEVER LET THAT GO IN VAIN.
MAY BE SOME OTHER WAY IT WILL COME TO YOU
AGAIN.
YOU MIGHT HAVE HAD A HEARTBREAK.
IT MIGHT HAVE CAUSED SOME HEARTACHE.
BUT GOD WILL HEAL ALL OF IT AND EVERY BIT.
HE KNOWS EVERYTIME WHAT YOU FEEL.
HE KNOWS EVERYTIME HOW YOU FEEL.
JUST BELEIVE HIM EVERTHING WILL HEAL.
ALL YOUR MISERY MIGHT BE DEEP.
YOU SOUL MIGHT WAIL AND WEEP.
BUT ONLY HE KNOWS THE CAUSE.
HAVE FAITH...THIS TOO SHALL PASS
HE IS THE REAL ONE TO HAVE YOUR CONCERN.
HE WILL REDUCE ALL OF YOUR BURDEN.
HE WILL GIVE YOU REWARD FOR YOUR MISERY.
AND ALL YOUR AGONY SHALL BURN.
HE KNOWS THE CAPABILITIES AND DISABILITIES.
HE HAS ALL YOUR GLORIES AND LIABILITIES.

HE KNOWS THE TRUTH AND UNKNOWN.
JUST BE STRONG AND FIRM.
HAVE FAITH AND PATIENCE.
IN YOUR BELIEFS AND IN YOUR LORD.
BECAUSE IT IS ONLY HIM WHO IS GREAT GOD.
HE IS MERCIFUL AND ABOVE ALL.
HE IS POWERFUL...YOU NEED TO RECALL.

55. ALL THE COURAGE.

Anxiety triggres and the fear pushes.
Tears flow and blood rushes.
My mind and heart.
My breath and soul.
Little they do cry these days.
Because now it all stays.
The pain and the misery.
The beauty and this scenery.
All together they create a story.
Little bit of courage cures all
the pain and damage.
All those tears turn into smiles.
All the miseries turn into glories.

56. JUST A LIE,

When you fall and you rise.
When you love you pay the price.
A fall that makes you wise.
A story that makes your life precise.
When you are hurt.
Your feelings all burnt.
The scars on the beautiful memories
The tears on all the tragedies.
Hold your stength I say...
Bear it with all the grace and dignity.
Accept it with all your will and serenity.
When you will be about to die.
Don't be upset that this life was just a lie.
Because even you knew it before your birth.
And now you will take this truth to death.

57. WHILE I WAS WAITING FOR YOU

WHILE I WAS WAITING FOR YOU.
I FORGOT YOU WERE A MERE ILLUSION.
WHILE I LOVED YOU TO THE EXTREME EDGE.
I FORGOT THAT YOU NEVER EXISTED.
WHILE I WAS DREAMING ABOUT YOU
DAY AND NIGHT.
I FORGOT I HAD MY LIFE TOO.
WHILE WRITING LETTERS FOR YOU.
I REALISED ALL MY WORDS ARE ONLY FOR YOU.
BUT YOUR WHOLE EXISTENCE IT WAS NOT
MEANT FOR ME.
YOU WERE JUST A THOUGHT A MIRAGE.
MERE BEAUTY OR MAY BE A DREAM.
WHILE I STARTED TO CONSIDER YOU EVERYWHERE
I FORGOT I HAD SOME CONSCIOUSNESS TOO.
BEING IN LOVE WITH YOU MADE ME
A MAIDEN'S BROKEN BANGLE.
THE SAME FRAGILITY AND VULNERABILITY.
WHILE SEARCHING FOR YOU EVERYWHERE.

I REALISED YOU WERE JUST AN ABSTRACT THOUGHT.

58. WORDS

All the pain and parts that are hurting.
I know everthing is reasserting.
Sometimes I feel afraid to give emotions to my words.
They feel like broken fragments from all my imaginations.
The words that I can't utter clearly.
The words that are written sophisticatedly.
And all the feelings along.
Can't take time to think so long .
Words resembling and alike.
The words that are fragile and even unkind.
The words that are honey at times.
And the words that might hurt like spines.
The words of love and hatred.
The words of dictation and division
All the words given emotions create the worlds.
The beginning and end all diffrent.
The nature and love its element.

59. TO THE JUVENILE MIND

LIVE THE LIFE WITH UTMOST ZEAL.
LET ITS ELIXIR YOU TO HEAL.
DON'T CRAVE FOR LOVE AND LIGHT.
FOR YOU, ARE ALREADY BRIGHT.
THE GLEAM AND CHARM.
AND YOUR SMILE QUIT WARM.
IT CAN FIGHT ALL THE EVENTS.
YOU HAVE THAT GRACE AND GLORY.
YOU HAVE AN EPIC STORY.
YOU DON'T NEED IMAGE FOR YOU.
YOU HAVE YOUR ART THAT YOU KNOW.
YOU HAVE THE HEART OF PURE ESSENCE.
YOU HAVE THE STRENGTH WHICH IS IMMENSE.
YOU ARE KIND TO ALL SO YOU WILL NEVER FALL.
YOU HAVE YOUR BOUNDARIES SET.
YOU HAVE YOUR LIMITATIONS UNKNOWN.
YOU ARE FREE AS A FLYING BIRD.
YOU ARE A BEAUTIFUL POET'S WORD.
ALL YOUR JUVENILE NATURE.
YOU ARE A MERCIFUL CREATURE.

THE BRAINS YOU HAVE GOT.
AND THE THOUGHTS YOU HAVE SOUGHT.
ALL YOUR LIFE IS GOING TO BE BEAUTIFUL.
YOU ARE ALREADY WONDERFUL.